Window on My World

Window on My World

By

Betty I Shipway

Date of Publication
January 2001

Published by
Ivy

© Copyright 2000 Betty I Shipway

Printed by
ProPrint
Riverside Cottage
Great North Road
Stibbington
Peterborough PE8 6LR

DEDICATION

This book is dedicated to the many friends made in the last 50 years.
To girls met during hospital training and in various hospitals who shared camaraderie and made difficult times tolerable. To those at Harefield Hospital 1952-1954 whose laughter salvaged life.
To other friends – Jen in Canada, for Joan and Jan whose friendships span 50 years and to Brenda who saved my life.
To God who gave me the gift of words and I hope my verses will give pleasure to others.
Betty J Shipway

CONTENTS:

Adolescent Love	1
A Day Given	1
Home	2
Portsdown Hill	3
Disillusionment in Friendship	4
Love's Delight	4
Violets in London	5
The Ward at Night	6
Richmond Hill	7
The Only Song	8
Arbor Vitae	9
City Blues	10
Wounded Mona Lisa	11
When Winter Comes?	12
The Snare of Love	13
Love Dying	14
I Beheld a Star	15
A Vision at Night -Time (St Martin's-in-the-Fields)	16
The Potential Copper Beech	17
July Night	18
Summer's Ending	19
Idyll of Flowers	20
Love Dead	21
Housewives' Lament	22
All in a Summer's Day	23
Our Youth	24
Evening at Appledore	25
Christmas (For Martin)	26
Where is He?	27
Lakeland Word Picture	28
Prayer for the Dying	29
Moon Landing	30
The Roads to God (Letter to an Adolescent)	32
The Turning Point	33
A Temporary Loss	34

Forest Paths	35
The Tyranny of Love	36
Crete	37
Dear Friend	39
Waiting for Death	40
Sounds of Summer	41
In Praise of Today	43
View From My Window	45
A Little Magic	46
Is There Anyone There?	48
The Bread of Life	49
Thanks Be to God	51
Dimanche a Alecon	52
Christian Take Heart	54
Country Cameo	55
Christian Does Thou See Them?	56
Cherry in Our Churchyard	57
The Flame of Freedom	58
Morning Comes	60
Peace in Our Time	61
The Return of Spring	62
From Death to Life	63
Sleep in Peace	64
Footprints in the Sand	65
The Chair	66
The Ultimate Dream	67
They Shall not Grow Old	68
Hope for the New Year	69
Summer's Anticipation	70
Death of a Princess	71
The Secret Garden	72
November	73
The Book of the World	74

ADOLESCENT LOVE

Wafting like cobwebs through clover-ridged fieldways,
Drifting as a spindrift on oceans high surge,
Stealing at night-time as starlight from Heaven,
Misting as moonbeams on evenings of gladness,
Breathless as a dance in fairyland given,
Whirling like leaves from autumn's russet treetops,
Gilded as lilies by waters of sadness,
Gay as all men at the dawn of fulfilment,
Holy as incense in Easter-clad chapels,
Quiet as streams through moors of mauve carpet,
Stormy at times a s a wreck tossed by waters,
Full of all magic, of strangeness, of wonder,
Of ways of all freedom and so is my love.

1947

A DAY GIVEN

By Fancies fed and Freedom's sound,
The key of Life and Joy is found,
The woodlane path, where green and fresh
Leaves stir, bound in gold spider's mesh.

The heathland slinks in purple guise,
Grey silence broods where shadow lies,
And minty ways and dusky scent
Help Nature in her Enchantment.

The foxglove sleeps, pale flowers glow;
Faint moonlight creeps, pale streamers show.
The night is bold, yet waiting still
As God's fingers creep over the hill.

1948
These are the first poems written aged 17 and 18 respectively.

HOME

Rustle of a gown gently dipping in the dew,
Murmur of bees, sigh of the wind in the May blue,
Pink hollyhocks, bending stately, lavender's scent,
All these old graces are vanished and as they went
Left only the low chime of the clock in the hall
Chiming the four – her portrait is hung on the wall
Grey gowned softly, with candles lighting her face,
Deep dark eye, a gracious smile and at her breast – lace.
Left only now is the spell of her tread;
Her limp dress in the closet and glowing red
Fire in her bedroom – a faint smell of her flowers.
Trees bend low; the sun in a red ball has no hours,
Left only now is the house where her love was found,
Her blessing is on it, her sweet magic has crowned
        our Home.

1948
To my dear mother who died in 1943 aged 36 and we didn't have a home, only a room and furniture in store.

PORTSDOWN HIL

Sea mist and autumn air and a city outspread,
Harbour lights pricking gently in a sheath of dim grey,
Bulbs glaring blatantly, in the distance their red
Is a myriad of stars in an earthbound Milky Way.
Traffic's night purr is muffled – men's voices are still.
A bus is a chariot, lighted with stars.
The magic spell of Olympus has taken my hill.
Moonlight glints below in silver bars,
On dark water where tumult and tide will not cease.
The faint silhouettes of mighty ships in the night
Tell of glad watching England and infinite peace.
So I calmly watch in the pale moonlight,
Feel the breath of God's air and the wonder of prayer.
Happiness, contentment of mind, for our land is secure.
Timeless spell of the sea, destruction cannot fare
Where glimpses of beauty are caught that are pure
In still sleeping air.

September. 1949

DISILLUSIONMENT IN FRIENDSHIP

You can pin your faith to a star in the sky,
To a purple mountain, a brook rushing by,
But with human kind, hope goes like a dream,
As summer sun dies beneath a new moonbeam,
Like the wide sea in the ebb and flow of the tide,
The dearest friendship is scattered far and wide,
And nothing remains but the illusion of trust,
It melts in dim time like a sigh in grey dust.

London January 1950

LOVE'S DELIGHT

Take one sweet sip of love's delight
And mix it with the music and the night
And the whirl of stars and moon will glow
In splendour on this earth and now
When morning's here, a night's unclouded dream will stay,
Remembrance tappings on eternity's day,
In spring-like madness, we will remain
Through laughing sun and cool winter rain.

London January 1950

VIOLETS IN LONDON

A flower stall in London's streets, a breath of home.
Rain tumbling down, a policeman's beat in town.
The cry of the streetman, the myriad lights that shine.
Taxi's horn, a piquant, laughing face
That brushes by, the whole dense roar of a London night,
And all above – lights!

By the corner tucked secure from garish glare
A flower stall stands, wreathed in carnations, hothouse plants.
Underneath and hidden, as if in hedgerow, violets show.

Out of town, Spring has come,
Buds blow, catkins are hung,
From the shimmering wet streets
The mind goes swiftly, seeing quiet night lit by stars.
The white gate – no cars
Rustle of trees, the birds' low song.
Like the bunch of violets, hope is gone.

London March 1950

THE WARD AT NIGHT

Shaded lights, quiet voices, stealthy footsteps here,
While the unseen watchers Death and Pain
Wait patiently:- one in I feel in horror as I sit near,
Pain, grinding, slow, unbearable torment for weak man,
Till death in proud majesty releases the old flesh,
Deep lines, plaintive, querulous cry are gone by
There remains the noble shell, while spirit
Seeks the realms of endless days and youth with bright wings is reborn.
A short span on earth and then away
To life eternal, clouds dreams, visions.

A4 Ward London Hospital
June 1950

RICHMOND HILL

Fresh September, sweet mist on bright grass and beauty
Far beneath, a glint of river, lights of leaping London town,
With what sweet magic – is the night – that night was crowned
With stillness, a wonder; peace brooded over our calm world,
Between the shadow of the trees, we disturbed deer
That crept stealthily to touch, while the proud stag
Reared; and stately stood, proud father of the night
A moment later he had gone, ghostlike, uncanny and the white
Mists rose; shadow covered the moon.
And the world stood still.

London September 22nd 1950

THE ONLY SONG

I'll have the wind for my fiddler,
The waves for my drum,
The leaves rustling softly guitar notes to strum.
I'll have a dream for a maestro,
The clouds for my score,
And that is what shall be my orchestra.

When the sun strikes the hill-top,
I'll have all my light
To tune up a merry tune far from the night,
A lark in the dawning will pick up my song
The splash of the merry stream
Will swing it along.

Somewhen about 1950

ARBOR VITAE

The weeping willow by the lake of sadness,
The swaying lilac with its breath of gladness,
Those signifying life in all its madness
When Spring wind blows.

While the spreading oaklands tell of security,
Life in the hidden hamlet with all its serenity,
While blue distant hills raise in clear purity
A ladder to Heaven.

The chestnut branches are candles to sacredness,
Scattering blossoms to earth to hide all its nakedness,
And soon all the earth is purged of all its lawlessness
And life has begun.

London 1950

CITY BLUES

Shine out the street light
Onto the wet, shimmering road.
The rays diffused by bucketing rain
Relentlessly pattering down.
The lights of the city flick on, flick off.
The London crowd rushes madly by.
Where are they all madly dashing to?
The hurry, the scurry, the bustle and noise.
All taking life at a tremendous speed.
Surrounded by others, you are alone
Walking slowly against the tide of hot humanity.

London 1950

All London poems written when a student nurse in a busy London hospital as an escape from loneliness.

WOUNDED MONA LISA

I see her in my daily work.
A dilapidated woman with ascites of the soul.
She sits unsmiling on her bed and rolls pathetic eyes,
And combs her long, straight hair; a Mona Lisa in disguise.
Her eyes are almond shaped with a glint of the insane.
Her complexion sallow and lips blue with pain
Of spirit; a miserable one who stands alone
From friendly, willing hands – she will sit and sigh and moan
And tell of what she was – a dancer long ago.
And she will stretch her long, thin legs and poise
Her toes in vain and contemplate her swelling belly full of woe.
And then she dreams of who she's seen and the noise
Of the cheering ones who acclaimed her dance,
Abandoned she will dance through tragedy and mirth.
Her slender figure will glide and turn and prance
And spin and swirl in draperies and leave the earth.
A gossamer figure fading into purple night
A queen of tragedy, a dying swan.
Pathetic, graceful, beautiful in white.
And then she wakes from reverie and finds her dream is gone.
She sits aloof and solitary, undesirable and cold.
But fascination lingers still and even with the breath of decay,
We still feel the wind of loveliness and the old
Sweetness of her body and the fragrance of May
In the dilapidated woman with the ascites of the soul.

Mrs Bailey, Medical Ward London Hospital
March 1951

WHEN WINTER COMES?

When the first of spring has cast its golden-tipped rays across
The first branch that lightly sways
And dips with fresh winds of March – when tossed
And shaken are the catkin boughs – we are amazed
That spring has come ; long winter days are passed.
And young new life will leap and throb and stay
To tide through the months that spring will last.
Alert, awake and blessed until the first of May.
Then sweet, white blossoms swell over the gate.
And night is heady with fragrant scents.
Intoxicated by this, we drift and dream and wait
And hope for better days on earth – rents
The mind of man and thinks he for that new Jerusalem,
Utopia, paradise and the rest – the idealist awakes
And sparks of God fill our world – and then why
When sunlight goes and the tree in amber shakes
Its leaves in anguish, do the dreams of men die?
Then only oblivion and self content and carelessness slip back;
Only spring and God and memory know their lack
When winter comes.

London March 1951

THE SNARE OF LOVE

In this sweet hellishness of mind.
Is love of body or of soul?
And why this twist and anguish felt?
And why in dreaming melt
In tenderness and longing for your nearness
And touch and spiritual dearness?
Akin to leap the planets, watch the moon
Spin in Heaven's timeless vault and too soon
Leave that delightfulness of mind where few men tread
Brought by your touch of physical awareness and led
By desire, flagrant and unscrupulous to want
And burn; and the mind is blanketed,
Obliterated – and I am lost with you.

London August 1951

LOVE DYING

Such thing is love existing not,
Save in the being of the mind
A face, the eyes, one imagineth
But know not.
The ideals are twisted with the time.
Invoking the beloved with rare qualities
So as to say a sunflower dyeth not,
And hath no seeds, no weeds, or unhid roots
The flower grows by the soil it feeds,
Like us no heavenly spark receives.

Hyde Park, London
September 1951

I BEHELD A STAR

When all others left me and I was desolate and alone
I took a walk at midnight into sleeping London town
I wandered by the riverside whilst snow slid gently down.
The wind was still, and I alone disturbed the night
With my footsteps. I hesitated by the bridge and white
And bare my world seemed. One star alone was there
Mirrored delicately in the icy blackness.
And wind blew up from nowhere.
I gazed intently, and borne on the wind a song
Burst forth:- 'Oh praise Him now, praise the Lord'
My mind swang back two thousand years,
I beheld the shepherds kneeling to the Holy child,
And Mary. Mother Mary with eyes so wise and mild.
The song of the angels swept the sky
While I gazed in wonder, and my eyes were not dry.

London Christmas 1951

A VISION AT NIGHT-TIME
St Martin's-in-the-Fields

I took a walk by the lonely sea,
While moonlight swept over sparkling spray.
And then a pathway clear was shown to me,
And while meditating there I saw my way.
The waters were divided and a path of light
Span towards the sand and white, warm
Fingers of desire, warmed my heart.
I saw the figure of our Lord peacefully part
Those waters bright – I fell on my knees in the sand
And bruised my knee – then raised by His hand,
As he passed down that radiant path, and still the sea did roar,
And I was alone with the presence of Christ upon that lonely shore.
And to my ears the singing came; bells and anthems raised
My soul, it left this puzzled earth and praised
With all men, through the open window of the sky
Came those voices from on high and rushing by,
This crazy world I glimpsed and saw the heartache nakedly
While the earth does fight and strive so blatantly;
Poverty of body and soul there, I knew how destitute we are,
And why our earthly bodies fade and how foolish men are.
I felt the pain of all the earth like His burden on my soul
But I swore by the stars and the silent night that God had made me whole
I heard the crying of the lost as discord in the night
And then the veil of glory shone and all the world was bright.
I saw stained glass windows standing clear against the morning light,
And heard the swell of the organ and a choir in all its might,
I saw a lane in springtime and a woman give a crust to a bird,
And I knew, that while flowers spring in sunshine
And dawn breaks in crimson beauty, that the voice of God is heard.

London Christmas 1951

The following four poems were written in Harefield recovering from TB caught whilst a student nurse in London.

THE POTENTIAL COPPER BEECH

While I lay in bed I watched spring come slowly,
A mother bearing gifts to Christ, loving but lowly,
The trees at first put forth delicate leaves,
A sparrow with fledglings built under the eaves.
Now in May a vista of green-ness appears; trees fling
Blossoms gently to earth, tantalising cuckoos sing.
Chestnut spires raise their candles, lit in the sunrise,
By red tinders of sky, saluting Minerva the wise,
A cedar stands staunchly, deep emerald leaves a foil,
For white petals, raised by the richness of a century's soil.
One tree only stood solitary, barren, aloofly unclad on the lawn,
Now has latent leaves tinted in the breaking red dawn,
A glowing copper, a sweet silver, a green light,
Proudly raising, etched clearly, a spell-binding sight.
Like an ugly duckling, grown swanlike, the trees stand at rest,
The last tree to blossom is the best.

Harefield May 1952

JULY NIGHT

Trees restly gently against a dim sky,
While a bright paper moon swings on high,
Quiet and peace…even the rooks are in bed,
But I am awake and delights round my head,
A dog calls sharply through the night,
And over the grass the dew falls white,
An avenue of trees lie away to the right,
In the country on a July night.

Overhead noisily a plane flies,
Over our lost citadel of sighs,
Strange nature's magic lingers still,
In the eye of the mind I climb a green hill,
While I idly watch a moth on the windowsill.
Then I walk by the river's way,
And smell the scent of new mown hay,
Just to wander where fields are wet
And then I shall forget, I expect.

Harefield July 1952.

SUMMER'S ENDING

The leaves of autumn falling,
Winter calling
Down the lanes,
Rain on window panes.
Tempestuous winds blow,
Heralding snow.
The garden is almost bare,
Black and sere.
Autumn woodsmoke's curling,
Birds fly southward wings unfurling,
Wheeling to the eternal spring.
Not a thing
Left; save a lonely robin's call
Alone and perky on the wall.

Harefield October 1952

IDYLL OF FLOWERS

Golden mimosa by my bedside,
Wavy in its golden fluffiness,
Was it plucked where warm winds blow?
Where a white house nestles in the stillness?
Picked by a dark-eyed laughing lady,
While her feet trod on golden flowers,
A handful of gilded mimosa glowing
By my bedside in December.

Then too, heather, smouldering richly
From pinecones scented,
Red as wine, or country madness,
Grown in peat, as minty sunrise.
Shining by a dim, dark pool,
Mirrored in the cool, deep depths,
Are the faces gone before us,
Shining there in tenderness.

Harefield January 1st 1953

LOVE DEAD

Strange my friend I swore I loved
Could have sworn it by the stars
Could have sworn by all I loved just you
But love died today, my love –
I look no more for your face in the crowd,
Or of the magical touch of you near,
For the you that was so warm
To me – is vanished – you are not dear
My love. For me the time has gone
I will search to love again no more
A fantasy; a breathless spell
Enchantment by music, yes the moon
Must have played her part, my dear
All the sweetness, savour gone
But now my soul's mine own,
Oh dear, my love.

Harefield October 1953

HOUSEWIVES' LAMENT

Let us escape the chains of reality,
Of washing up, of washing down,
Sunday lunch, the hoovering,
Run wild in the fields without a care,
Capture spring, and not spring cleaning,
Turn husbands back as erstwhile lovers,
Smoke in bed, regardless of carpet holes,
Drink coffee late, heedless of the school run,
Enjoy our children and their brightness,
Not caring whether teeth are cleaned or shoes unbrushed.
Turn back the clock, be adventurous
We seem to be so careful now,
Who once ran laughing in the rain.
Watch the budget – shoes outgrown,
Why is the telephone bill so exorbitant?
Surely the car will last forever.
Let us escape the chains of reality,
And greet the spring with arms outstretched.
Somewhere – a minute away escapism lies,
Not far – sometimes an eternity it seems.

Spring 1966

ALL IN A SUMMER'S DAY

Morning comes today washed in brightness
The yachts that run to meet the dawn,
Glide silently into the whiteness
Of a peaceful summer's day
And melt into the skyline.

The cornfield stands in splendour
Too dazzling for the eye,
Scarlet poppies shout a welcome,
To the blue glory of the sky
A skylark sings.

The lazy pond in summer lies,
The kingcups incline their kingly gold,
And over all the iridescent dragonflies
Speed and zoom to bless the day,
Shimmering in heat.

By a stream a small boy sits
Clad in faded jeans,
Languidly plying for a fish
Nearby his mongrel dog leans
Panting by a log.

On the river bank two lovers meet,
Stealing then a kiss,
Till the bright day fades once more,
Into quiet and river mist.
The wind stirs.

By the sea night has come
Quietly after a brilliant sunset.
The waves still barely lap onto the shore,
The tide – the sand and night well met,
Dissolve into a purple oneness.

Summer 1967

OUR YOUTH

Was it us in days of youth,
Gaily undertaking mountains?
Nothing seemed unobtainable then.
The world our plaything
For the asking – Heaven sent.
Strange how youth has left its footprints,
Encompassed now with little things,
It is the small things which are highlights,
Things so natural one remembers,
Births and deaths and loving wishes.
The earth does not shake and tremble,
Sometimes still the flash of insight,
Remote, away from earthling pleasures,
A brief glimpse of ultra senses,
Thus the way all time it passes.

May 1968

EVENING AT APPLEDORE

Sunlight glinting on water blue,
Seagulls swirling,
Wings unfurling,
Sailboats gliding,
Speedboats flying.
The gentle lap of tide on tide.
Peace and quiet now,
Ratrace discarded.
Vague sweet mews of seagulls calling,
With what joy tranquillity descending,
The mind broken, nearly, nearly mending.

August 1968

CHRISTMAS
For Martin

This was the tale of the Christmas rose
Of the Christ who came to ease our woes,
Now Christmas time is tinsel time with present joys.
And happy times for girls and boys.

There is the tree with laden greenness
Sparkling with bobbles and shimmeringness
There are the parcels giving great excitement
The children all on happiness intent.

After lunch the grownups sit and yawn
The family united since Christmas morn.
They may perhaps have had family prayer
Do they remember why they are there?

Remember the star which led the wise men on.
The ray of hope, which is the dawn.
The Christ who came a child on earth,
To give us all a glad new birth.

Christmas 1968

WHERE IS HE?

Why do they bother to look for the moon?
The world will come to an end too soon,
Why do they strive to reach the stars,
Or send mighty rockets up to Mars?
Life is at best a fleeting time,
The hair that was black will soon turn to rime.
Life is now, is joy, is giving,
Savouring the moment, begetting and living.
The world has lost the essential things,
Like listening while a skylark sings.
Are they looking for God up there?
Foolish man – God is here.
Our world is crowned with materialistic light
There seems nothing good will come out of this fight.
Our brother man lies starving, dying,
While we look aside and heed not his crying.
We spend our time acquiring possessions,
While a small minority just make confessions.
Why can't we get back to the spirit of life?
Why all the fighting and all the strife?
At birth we're given the blessing of Heaven,
Why throw it away before we are seven?
Few people left will reach up for God,
Yet He is nearby us from birth to the sod,
A living reality of man, reborn,
Offering us again Life! On Easter morn.

January 1969

LAKELAND WORD PICTURE

These mountains have stood for the lost centuries past,
Alert, watchful, majestic, solitary.
Heeding not men's wild ways, nor yet his worry.
Wreathed sometimes in white mist, swirling and changing,
Cloudcapped at times, now sombre, now smiling.
In colours black, brown, russet, green, ochre and grey,
Greyly substantial and encircling lakeland.
While white snow in hidden gullies lingers long.
To climb them struggle, heartache, longing,
To conquer – beauty – grandeur, solemn wonder,
While ghylls that run to sunlit valleys thunder.
The sheep on hillsides idly graze and often stray,
Their green fields divided by neat, grey stone walls.
High up lie the crofters' hut grey and solid,
Woven all into pastoral kaleidoscope.
Little springs spring and dash and bubble merrily
To join formation with gay, sparkling rivers
Which in turn enjoin the ever constant lakes,
Whose colours change with sun and everlasting sky.
Below a sleeping paradise of colour.
Latent rain bringing clear freshness to the eye.
Greens are greener, yellows golden, reds scarlet;
Each small leaf glistens wetly in the sunlight.
Each lake quivers reflecting cloud formation,
Sweet scents and bird song add to grand profusion.
Colour, sound, smell, vision awaken all the senses.
Blended all into tranquil scenes, no confusion.
Above the lakes, pine trees lay on gentle slopes.
Dark green, light green, like sentinels they stand,
Leading onwards to the brooding high mountains,
Beyond each peak another peak looms,
Till grey clouds and grey mountains reach
One fusion…

May 1969

PRAYER FOR THE DYING

I do not want to look at the world of pain,
The dim, dark lights or the strumming rain.
How can you say to those who suffer so;
'Hold my hand and it will go'?
How can you say to them who suffer hell
'Time is the healer – time will tell'?
they say 'You know I'm dying nurse'
You laugh it off and inwardly curse.
Can you say? – Oh of course you should -
'This is the long and terrible wood;
Beyond the snares and the roots and the tangled thorn,
Your soul will soar like a bird at dawn'
How can you tell them? Each lie in their imprisoned shell,
You know they fight the pain which is hell.
God! Can't you help them, give them peace?
Tell them pain will one day cease,
Help their minds give their body ease,
Why can't the body give the soul release?
So they can smile before they die,
Listen to their plaintive cry!
Death is the only friend you send;
Peace will then on them descend.
How to tell them – this is the test,
To tell them death will give them rest.

Basing Road Hospital June 1969

MOON LANDING

So they finally landed on the moon,
Dispelling the mystic century's old charm,
They planted in grey lunar dust
The stars and stripes to forever stand .
And peered at the bleak, still moonscape
Looks at cubic rocks where no erosion shapes.
It is indeed a great, scientific wonder,
An engineering feat beyond compare.
Will moondust rate a billion dollars
In the markets of the world?
Rarer than gold with more potential than gas?
What strange and wondrous elements there,
Will moonshine help this world to care?
Perhaps miraculous cures we'll have,
Perhaps the dust of eternal life,
Will it still this earthly strife?
Or was it just a scientific dream,
Realised at last? Yet giving little.
Have we lost the magic of it all?
The madness – moonbeams – silly things
And just revealed a lost strange world
Desert of grey dust and craters void.
Only time will and it won't care.
Will placards read – 'Holidays on the Moon'
1,000 dollars down! The rest in instalments.
The adventure of your life! 'No Fishing'

Collect your tickets and leave your wife.
'Rest in the Sea of Tranquillity'
excavations to moon craters daily
Five gallons aviation fuel – two cokes please.
Dollars the only accepted currency
Ice cubes only given to millionaires,
Leave behind earth with all its cares.
As we have said before time will tell
Our descendants will reap the breathless spell
Of this year's landing on the moon.

July 20th 1969

THE ROADS TO GOD
Letter to an Adolescent

There are many roads to God, my dear,
The way is not always shining clear.
Some reach to the cathedral of the sky
And see it as a star on high.
They find it in nature's wonderment,
And so find out that life's not ill-ment.
For some the torn and twisted way:
And some find it only when they pray,
Others maybe tossed and wracked with fear,
Then cry out to God and find him near.
For many the pageantry and song.
This may seem trite but it's not wrong.
Take away the trappings if you must.
Put out your hand and in His word trust.
See him as the creator…steadfast friend,
Individual ways lead to the same end.
Condemn not others, in the way of the young,
Listen still while the Amen is sung.
The ways are all devious, my dear,
You'll find your own one day, so do not fear.

For Gillian 1970

THE TURNING POINT

Shall we venture to lands anew?
And see the stars in a different view,
Shall we chance it, take the plunge
Away from the whole familiar scene.
Leave the serenity of what we are
And take a look at what might have been
A vast new world of different things,
Change the way of life – be adventurous.
Turn the whole world upside down – literally
Can we turn back the clock so flippantly?
Security, our age group strives for?
Is that enough our souls to cry for?
We need fresh sensations, need our dreams,
While our minds still active pursue these things.
We had better take the chance and now,
Before the cocoon of middle-aged complacency
Takes us! Before we lose the wanderlust.

Anyhow enough to say, we stayed in England with some advantages and some disadvantages.

February 1970

A TEMPORARY LOSS

Down the long winding road I lost it.
It was not lost in entirety,
But it shattered
And fragments fell like snow
Along the road of misfortune,
So I remain feelingless,
Incapable of laughter or sorrow,
Shell-like now which was effervesced
The droplets bubbled then,
Spilled over with life.
So once was gaiety and song,
Subsiding into tears and smiles,
Now seems barren,
Smothered on the treadmill
Of the commonplace.
I see snowflakes falling
Along the line of pines
And the sunlight calling
Still no response –
It seems a grey world.
Perhaps the glint of daffodils
And thrusting life of spring
Will refresh and renew my soul.
Or am I doomed forever
To wander in the middle mist?

February 1973

FOREST PATHS
Simile on Depression

I do not want to wander thus
Down the wandering path
Which bends and twists and darts and turns
Into bog and mud and damp, dark pools.
It leads nowhere but to fear and despair.
The sun grows cold and light fades
Into fog and dying bracken crunches
Underfoot.

More stumbles and halts and desolation
Trees now stripped and stark
The road to self destruction and guilt.
We will sink into a morass of hesitation
Self doubt and retribution.
The bog will claim us both
Damp and blank and leave us
Without trace.

Let's take the other straighter way,
Without the endless twists and turns,
It leads straight off the major road
Open and clear and positive –
The views are crystal clear and fine,
So the bracken still is dead,
But enshrined all in spider's web
Which glistens.

We may have fallen tree trunks there,
Visible clearly in the autumn sun,
Step over these obstacles
And laugh! For they are none.
It is an easier way by far,
Happier too, less complicated.
Step freely and with confidence
On this path.   *October 16th 1980*

THE TYRANNY OF LOVE

So close, so far,
So near, so dear.
Like a spider's web it clings.
Enmeshed forever in a strand,
At times it gives the helping hand.
At times the bitter sweet command.
Sometimes rope-like with tightened band
Then freedom calls,
The mesh enthrals
No way it seems for liberty
The web destroying thee and me.

November 1980

CRETE

Intrude not here, just observer be,
Of blue Cretan skies, land of the olive tree,
Tread warily: for this is ancient land,
Where golden mimosa blows!
The people dark-skinned clinging to their past,
Leading quiet lives unblemished yet,
By 20th century's hectic pace.
Industriously and quietly pursuing pastoral ways.
Weaving, milking goats, tending the vine,
As always donkey riding.
With its scent of sage, pungent and pure,
While sun beats down on rocky slopes and shore.
There is a timeless quality of life,
For generations before have kept simple lives
In touch with living Gods.
Lassithi's plain lies like another world
And from the villages spread-eagled there
Church bells ring out in still and quiet air,
The white walls shimmer in sunlight's magic spear.
While clouds on mountains rise in white,
Giving unity with earth.

So did the Gods once stride these heavens?
And if so – are they still there?
So look at Zakros – desolate now,
But still those ancient people's spirit stays.
It seems like the end of the world,
But not, for it was the beginning then,
When proud Minoans sacrificed the bull,
And lived and breathed.
As seen by Knossis splendid shell,
How great they were, magnificent in life,
And confident in death of future glories and eternity.
Remember them – the mighty ones!
So far away – this lovely flower-filled isle,
From our bright new world
Of lights and comfort and modern brashness
It has captured time itself
Imprisoned it in sunlight and bound it
With the olive tree of. Peace.

April 1981

DEAR FRIEND

The candle burning brightly
Has expired.
Which flickered softly
Has left its glow
On earth.
So when memory awakes,
It will be of laughter.
We recall.
Of happy days and singing
Of the brave spirit.
We must not mourn and
Think of what could have been,
For God has taken you to rest
From pain and suffering.
Au Revoir dear friend
In advance of us you go
To greet your maker in the sun.

For Anne-Marie April 17th 1982

WAITING FOR DEATH

Will you come as a thief in the night
To take my last unguarded breath?
Or will it be on the wings of morning
With brightness and hastening on?
I do not fear you, old grey Reaper.
The friend of all mankind in the end.
For I am so very tired of pain,
So tired of trying, of struggling on.
I have had a good, hard fight in life,
And mostly got the ends tied up.
I think I've touched the highs and lows,
Had loves, and laughs and walked on snow,
High in the mountains – God is there.
So when this body, tired and worn
Is gone, the essential me will still be here,
Not dull and drowsy, with pain and drugs,
But alert and caring to essential joys.
No mourning, please for me,
But happy hymns and pleasant thoughts.
Please God give me absolution from my sins,
Bless my nearest with the eternal hope
Of resurrection and give us the peace,
Which the world cannot give.

November 1st 1983

SOUNDS OF SUMMER

How blest the sounds of summer long,
The dawn chorus starts with one bird's call,
Then all around they awake and shout;
Sounds good, the echoes from high trees,
To one who knows its staking territorial claim.
'Hands off, it's mine, this nest is not for sale!'
Soon rustle in the trees, as squirrels come,
Tame, too adventurous by far and even they
Gymnasts supreme, make branches sway.
Then use their plume of tail to balance high.
While Tom the cat, in anger waits for them to drop
Onto his patch below.
Later as the sun rises high in cloudless blue,
The bees come alive and swarm the syringa by garden wall.
The eager thrush comes hop-tapping on the lawn,
While supine cat opens one green eye and yawns,
Too languid to move, with ears attuned like antennae
To sounds; another cheeky bird calls the alarm cry loud.
His noise so loud from that tiny frame,
Out of all proportion is his sound.

Still summer sounds are bliss indeed.
Even with the children's cries and the raucous ice-cream man,
Who insists he plies his trade,
With just a hint of summer sun.
Peace mostly except for birds and bees,
Whose industry could rule our world.
Till evening comes and after neighbour's mower's hum,
The rooks in haste and noisily to high nests repair –
The sun has gone, in blaze of glory to rest,
But summer sounds still abound,
For Tom the cat is now alert and all nocturnal
Things are on the prowl.
The barn owl will glide and swoop and turn.
And so to bed for human kind,
The summer day vanishing like a wisp of cloud.
Only left the scent of honeysuckle by the porch,
Encaptured on wind, to attract the vagrant moth.

Written in the garden, Croft Road
July 5th 1984

IN PRAISE OF TODAY

With all the gloom and doom and dire despair,
I'll sing a song of praise and comfort.
The switch of the switch, the turn of the screw;
The opening of the mighty can.
For this is today.
Our conveniences have given us freedom
To think; perhaps too much,
But reflect;
For us, we miss the shadows of the flickering fire,
We also miss the icy draughts of ice cold,
Which invaded passages from room to room,
We miss the long excursions to the privy,
With candlelight held in fear of bats at night.
We sleep at night in warmth.
No more the icy morning, with our breath before us yawning
In white mists.
So it snowed last night.
We miss the frost flowers on window panes,
We also miss chilblains, and the feverish dressing in bed,
Before we put the reluctant foot,
Into the cold morning of bleak mid-winter.

Aside from this and for myself,
For thrice has Death called me on his rolecall,
And thrice has been eluded by the modern drug;
So I met him eye to eye and laughed.
In past days the grave would long ago have claimed myself;
And I would never have known the joys that come with travel.
In youth one read the National Geographical
In quiet, musty library, in mittens,
Dreaming of other lands, and people,
But today, we realise our dreams of childhood –
And see and feel and experience it firsthand,
The mountain tops and walk on snow, above the valleys.
The air thin, but pure and unpolluted.
How marvellous, what grandeur there,

Even better than books, the true reality.
We board the plane, itself a wonder,
And travel fast, static it seems,
And view clouds below, in fantastic formation,
While we are bathed in the eternal sun.
Dropping down the islands show,
Like blotting paper in a silver sea.
Or otherwise we go, and visit ancient Rome.
Better than dreams, again, the reality of this…
The mightiness of empires gone,
And put a foot where the almighty past was once,
In cool colonnades, in ruins now,
So treading on the past, history seems but a moment gone.
For how could our forebears know these joys?
It was then the lot of common man
To work and toil, begat and die –
For most not even compensation of the written word.
So we, the inheritors of past peasants' lot,
Should take our pleasure now, and not forget,
The hardships past and poverty stark.

We are informed by radio, and by T.V.
Of other peoples, other lands,
Perhaps we see other nations rising;
To claim creature comforts and freedom of thought and word,
And why not? Providing these inanimate things,
Became the tools, and not the Gods of men –
Therein the danger lies; we are poised on the brink –
'A little learning is a dangerous thing'
That's true – for we should have the sense,
To use science for our own end and rejoice
In the freedom of our choice,
And choose wisely; and not tempt
Our own annihilation.

February 9th 1985

VIEW FROM MY WINDOW

The whole village lies asleeping
The winter long its vigil keeping –
Although the sun has long since risen
In cold, red ball in heaven,
It sheds no warmth on us below,
And does not melt the white, impacted snow –
A few birds solitary do call,
For winter's hands have petrified us all.
The roofs of houses lie in white,
The occasional plume of smoke in sight,
Sounds are muted, traffic is still,
The coldness saps our very will –
Trees are stark, with snow still lying
On bare branches; they seem dying,
But we know that spring will come,
And all will thrive, which still seems numb.

To prove that I can still make the rhyme.
Croft Road, Oakley February 15th 1985

A LITTLE MAGIC

Spring came today, in haste and prematurely,
And flung its gauntlet, at the icy blasts,
That had swept over us continually,
For yet amongst the grasses, high, lies
The ice, still unmelted by the sun.
We glimpsed 'The Dreaming Spires'
For once in balm blue gown
The sky, not crying as before –
But now benign, it glowed.
The heron soared by the Isis there,
While privileged youth sped by in boats,
It is now the joy of winter gone,
For lovely youth will have its day.
The coaches vigorously ride in glory, on their bikes,
Young men, drinking great gulps of life,
And girls as well, with gentler strokes,
Bullied all, by the little ones, crouched,
Encouraging, extolling, shouting in the stern,
'On, on, to victory, you lot!'
'Together, men . three, two one and go…'
One female coach, with blonde hair flying,
A young Venusm risen, with perfect form
Of rounded youth, was loudly crying.
Urging young men to better feats,
For like a Goddess, she appeared,
Although in shorts and unadorned
Her charisma shone, her crew would win the heats.

The runners came, along the path, panting, sweating in the sun,
And one stood out, Apollo like,
With body beautiful and muscles taut,
A golden youth, embodiment of them all,
As yet no blemishments to mar,
No sears of life, to mark his fall,
Along the towpath, the ordinary mortals walked,
With babes in chariots, gurgling in the warmth,
While numerous dogs, ran in the cool water,
And smiled, and panted, shaking droplets everywhere,
Today the magic's in the air,
For youth and spring together cling,
The river lending a happy time to man,
Its placid progress enlivened by the eager youth,
And so it achieved a different span.
It was idyllic there that day,
If only youth and sun and love could stay.

Oxford February 24th 1985

IS THERE ANYONE THERE?

'Is there anyone there?' she said
When alone, with clouds of domesticity rolling round her head,
The children flown the nest, passions now at rest.
'Shall I make the jam? Pick the apples?
Mow the lawn, or just relax and dream?'
So if alone, don't pause to think
Until the knot inside, expands and grows,
Was it all in vain, where are the busy, fruitful years?
All gone and melted in time's melting pot –
In the past the wheel span round relentlessly.
No time to ponder on the essential ego
The little core of every personality
Was ever swamped by other's needs –
Now the wheel has stopped, wound down
And there is time to spare
Now is the once longed for peace.
But now alone, she ponders on her ease,
Looking inwardly and with some despair,
'I look inside' she says
      'Is there anyone there?'

Margaret
October 1985

THE BREAD OF LIFE

'Follow me' He said as He stood by the silver sea,
'Follow me' it will not be an easy path
To follow, feet will weary, legs will ache,
Salvation will be given for thirst to slake,
Love will sustain as bread to take,
'For I am the giver of life' said he;
'Take up your cross and follow me!'

'The gifts I give are not of this earth,
peace I send and joy I bring
and healing from all suffering.
But you must foremost love your God,
And then love your fellow men' he said.
How simple both these commandments read,
Taking no account of man's all-consuming greed,
Our world is in a sorry state,
Much poverty of soul today –
Difficult to bring the gift of peace,
When violence does never ceases,
Difficult in these enlightened times,
When science rules our hearts and minds.
For man has achieved advancement here,
Forgetting The Creator who was there,
Forever and forever more.
His power greater than the petty human brain,
His knowledge deeper than the sea,
Open wide my heart that I may find –
The deeper love than human kind.

I saw Him walking by the sea,
With arms outstretched saying 'Follow me',
So when our group was full of prayer,
There was no doubt that He was there.
Please help us in our difficult, doubting hour,
To always feel the everlasting power,
And love given freely on the cross.
'Follow me, drink this in remembrance of me'
He said 'Understand with your heart and not with your head',
Please guide us in whatever path we are led.
And when our first Communion bread we break,
It will be The Bread of Life we take.

Confirmation
February 24th 1987

THANKS BE TO GOD

We thank Thee for spring rain that falls,
For slanting sun and hint of daffodils,
We thank Thee for our teacher, friend –
Who showed us your way, world without end –
Guide her in her holy ministry,
So your word will spread like the latent apple tree,
For first the seed and then the tree,
Will stand garlanded for Thee,
Who now hides its blossom waiting there,
And later still its fruit will bear,
And so to our teacher, friend we pray,
Blessings on your pilgrim way,
Lift high the cross,
The love of Christ proclaim,
Till all the world,
Adore his sacred name.

For Marjorie Honnor
March 1987

DIMANCHE A ALENÇON

The bells ring out their welcome call,
Calling over the grey, slated roofs
Of high houses, bereft of their medieval wall,
Peering onto narrow, cobbled streets,
Bidding attendance to Notre Dame èglise.
'Come celebrate Communion with us all
On this sparkling morn of song'.

Yesterday the market place beside the church
Was vibrant with life and ablaze with colour,
With mingling patois of country folk,
Selling their wares to the sophisticate
Of the town, oh so polite to sell and serve
The flowers of every shape and hue.
Stalls laden with apples, peaches. Pears,
Courgettes, melons – aubergines and grapes.
What cheeses! Roquefort, camembert and brie,
There's fish and fowl, oysters as well.
Everyone chatters and gesticulates
For this was Saturday's market morn
In the sun, in Alencon.

Now Sunday is here!
Ring out your bells in joyous note,
Call French brother and Englishman together –
For our roots are intertwined by war –
Although long ago we fought as foes,
Now brothers clasped by liberty's hour.
More than 40 years on we remember still,
Normandy fields where poppies grow
Scarlet; blood of blood of brother lies
Together; under the wide unchanging sky of France.
There is still the pollarded polar tree
In straight avenues, leading to the sea.
Where once long ago William came
To conquer England – but now
The sea, which was once the enemy
Is now the route to unite us all
'Vive La France' we say and you in return
Will say 'Vive L'angleterre. J'Espere'.

Alençon September 25th 1987

CHRISTIAN TAKE HEART

Christian, take heart,
We all have our part,
Sometimes we see through glass of dark,
We seem to lose our little spark.
Sometimes the veil is lifted high,
Revealing the glory from the sky.
We see the radiance of the cross,
Showing its pathway for the lost.
So clear and bright and simple it shines.
Shattering the complexities of our minds.
Doubts, fears, tortures are swept away
You are with us when we pray –
Do not despair, you have glimpsed the glory there.
And although the vision seems to recede,
And pilgrimage is tough indeed,
Remember the vision you have seen.
The eternal city stands serene.
And Christ will extend His hand to you,
And His love will guide you through.
It seems man cannot sustain the vision bright.
The celestial prospect too dazzling for our sight.
So look as well in the human race,
For the glimpse of the Spirit in another's face.
So Christian do not despair,
Human frailties we all share.

1987

COUNTRY CAMEO

The picture is hung in the tiny hall,
By the grandfather clock in the cottage small,
Where sunlight slants and shines on its still face,
It tells of summers gone and faded lace.
A country scene comes alive to the gaze,
There are gleaners bending in the golden haze.
With pink bonnets shaded against the sun
And racing rabbits seem once again to run.
An indolent youth lies in faded blue
Recumbent, is he whistling a tune or two?
There is the haycart, overloaded with hay
Where rosy children's faces shine in sunlight's ray.
As they peer over the top with mischievous smiles
And stretching before them for miles and miles
The golden corn glows, and poppies shout
Welcome; to all who are out and about.
A group of old men with pipes in hands
Sit on stacked bales, their britches covered in tiny strands
Of wafting straw and as old men are want t do,
They talk of their past, when their world was new.
This picture has captured a moment in time.
Standing still in the ripe summer sunshine.
The figures are at one with nature's hand,
Indivisible from the welcoming land.

February 1988

CHRISTIAN DOES THOU SEE THEM

Christian beware!
For with hands held high and head in air,
You reach the bell ropes and pull
High in the belfry tower are you!
Keep your feet upon the ground
As you ring your peel of bells.
For the light of the world is for all mankind.
See the sun, its splendour shines for all,
Feel the rain, refreshing flowers and earth,
Likewise the cross, its message is given clear
To you; so what are you going to do?
This is not an elitist club you know,
For see them with their suppliant hands.
For they are all your fellow men,
Needing kindness, tender loving care,
Not calling to the empty air,
'For you must love your fellow men'
He said; 'and show them the radiance of the cross',
But softly then, for you do not know the pain they bear,
Open you ears and you may hear,
Keep your feet upon the ground
But step by step the way is rough,
But sure this is the road to take,
With happiness for His name's sake,
Heeding all the travellers on the way,
And helping them to learn to pray.

After the vision of the Bells in the Belfry
1988

CHERRY IN OUR CHURCHYARD

Scatter the blossoms over the ancient graves,
For there it is a thing of beauty,
With its branches laden with blossom,
With sweet, white petals like white tears,
As it grows and blooms and grows
Over the Christians gone before,
In other centuries gone by.
Inside we talked of our shepherd king,
Who said to follow as His lambs,
As white, white flocks of purity
Glowing in our world.
And there he stands in raiment white,
Calling us to follow His voice –
As a sacred lamb, He came.
And we glimpse briefly, so briefly,
The ever present bounty of His love.
It is all bound up with the tree of life
On this spring morning, and the blossoming
Cherry, captures the faith of Christ
Sheltering the ancient graves with white petals,
Soon its tears, like pearls will fall silently
Giving your benediction to those at rest.

St. Leonard's Churchyard, Oakley
April 1989

THE FLAME OF FREEDOM

Autumn leaves flutter over the ancient, slanting gravestones,
November sun glows on this day –
Onto the village church and around
For God is smiling on this day.
A day of symbolism and peace on earth.
A remembrance day for the departed dead –
Whose bodies lie sleeping deep in Flander's fields,
On Normandy plains, in ancient Crete.
Those known only to God at rest.
Whose blood given, shows only in poppy fields,
Where lines of white crosses are bathed in sun,
The old men walk with measured tread,
But proud, with medals of past campaigns
Winking on their red breasts –
It as yesterday to them and God
When brave, young men carelessly gave their lives
For patriotism, and for their ideals.
Cry freedom! 'We shall fight on the beaches'
And they did – they shocked the sky
With soaring, mangled bits of steel,
They filled the ocean with debris,
And spread their bodies in the deep.
Just for peace and for a brave new world.
Remember them, they gave their lives for us.
So now the swirling poppies fall
On the young, unlined faces of today.
(But in the graveyard God sends his flame of autumn leaves)

But this year is different, miraculous indeed...
While we remember them, down goes the wall,
God is smiling on this day.
30 years of bitterness and pain
Has been swept away, dis integrated –
The smiling faces shine and young and old together
Burst out with joy and their tears
Of happiness wash out the pain
Of all past grievances and lost hopes.
Should we in future years let scarlet poppies fall
In remembrance of that horrific wall?
Or let God send his autumn leaves to fall?
As in that quiet graveyard, wreathed in peace,
Remember them, remember Him, the Prince of Peace
Who gave His life that we might live
For God is smiling on this day.

St. Lawrence Churchyard
November 1989

MORNING COMES

I have seen the beauty of the morning,
Bright with the smile of December sun.
Still the village lies sleeping
But sunrise shows the day begun.

In somnolent gardens, frost is white on the lawn.
The trees stand stark, in the morning light,
Birds call briskly, already risen to greet the dawn,
Fir trees, feather erect, are veiled in white.

The cottages and houses in the lane
Are window blinded, still unaware
That morning calls on their window pane,
Just feel the vibrant, joyous air.

As I walk the first man appears,
The paper boy, still vaguely yawning,
The old man with a dog, both old in years,
Saying so brightly a gay 'Good morning'.

Down to the duck-pond where fierce activity and noise
Shatters the stillness with comic cry,
For they are alert and in mating poise,
But the cottages around in slumber lie.

Soon all the village will awake from sleep,
And will be filled with the busyness of the human race,
So thank you God for another God given day, where winter sun
gives benediction to this place.

Oakley Village Sleeping
December 1990

PEACE IN OUR TIME

'Pray for peace', they say,
God send peace on our troubled world…
I see the earth spin in a timeless vault of Heaven –
Like the globe of childhood's memory,
It spins unsuspended in a blue void.
To the right the cross on high,
Shedding its light towards the earth,
Brilliant, illuminating, penetrating.
Look again, a shadow around the globe,
The continents and the seas are covered in mist.
The mist portrays the endless struggle of mankind,
For the greed of man blankets the earth.
The long time forces of evil and good
Once more enacting, once more at play –
God send your light to dispel the mist.
For there is our world of mountain peaks,
And mighty rivers rushing to the sea,
Beautiful. Majestic, unobtainable…
While men rush around like ants,
Preparing for war, caught up in chaos,
While starving children cry for bread,
And the affluent worship materialism,
No wonder the world is shrouded in mist.
So God who causes nature's voice to thunder
Send your cross of light with power
To dispel the shroud that covers earth…
Give us your gift of Peace and more,
Help us to wipe away the tears of the world.

January 11th 1991

THE RETURN OF SPRING

Hold your breath – the new day is dawning,
The sun dispels the mists of morning,
Silently, imperceptively she comes
The earth again stirs and mantles
Everywhere with green; the living world
Again renewed with the miracle of spring.
For now the forsythia's a golden haze,
And the daffodils a golden blaze.
Now the cow presents a white-faced calf
Who lurches insecure on new-born legs.
And lambs' heads butt with sheer delight,
And the blackthorn bush is garlanded with white.
Capture the moment, life's for living,
God has given – we should be praising.
So thank God for this heaven sent day
Now the earth is stirring; to yield once more
The tender shoots of May.

March 1993

FROM DEATH TO LIFE

The ceaseless mobility of death appals us,
Leaves us lost on a common treadmill –
Spring, summer, autumn, winter are our lot,
We are shattered by its inevitability –
But we should know and know we must,
Living faith will raise us from the dust.
Spirit calling spirit, a never ceasing flow
From earth to heaven; the anthems raise
Songs burst forth; the light is bright,
And angels sing with endless praise,
Life ending is just a beginning,
Our limiting minds cannot comprehend
The vastness of eternity –
Where reigns one King of Kings,
One redeemer of all mankind –
Who carried a cross for everyone –
So we may reach heaven with fingertips,
Immortality granted and peace provided,
Rest in peace, Pip

March 1994 For Pip

SLEEP IN PEACE

Sleep in peace,
The world disguarded,
Sleep…unreguarded
Waiting for eternity to call you,
The shimmering stars to own you,
Then walk towards the celestial light.
The Holy Spirit will guide you,
The Prince of Peace will call you,
The Heavenly King will claim you.

Somewhen in 1994

FOOTPRINTS IN THE SAND

Brave men marching, brave men singing –
At a distance young and hearty –
Close up shows the toil of years,
50 years on, they march jubilante

Honouring comrades gone before them
Then there was no band to lead.
Just an inner strength to guide them,
And a touch of fear and brave defiance.
Patriotism burned then so brightly,
They were the chosen to end tyranny –
Ordinary men inspired by flames of freedom,
With perhaps a lone piper calling
As they landed, cold and wet and seasick,
Determined, young and pretty reckless,
Sometimes a friend would fall beside them,
And lie in the wet sand motionless,
While soul with bright wings
Joined the army not forgotten
Of countless others dead in battle –
Waiting for the Last Post to call them.
So the brave old men were marching
On the sands at Arromanchis.
Honouring their comrades gone before them,
Honoured by the highest in the land.
Tears were shed of humility and pride,
Pride of our nation, pride in those men,
Leaving their footprints in the sand.

50th Anniversary of Normandy Landings on T.V.
June 7th 1994

THE CHAIR

Enter the room quietly,
With hushed and solemn tread,
He is not there but spirit lingers yet,
The books, the mugs, the plants
All invoking memories of times past.
Cushions and rugs falling carelessly
Onto much worn sofas.
There's the picture bought many years ago
Of an estuary in Devon – happy days!
And there's his chair!
Waiting for him to sit peacefully,
Reading, relaxing with a multi-coloured cat.
How can you tell a cat of death?
Although a cat must know, being perceptive,
Wary, and knowing all things,
From an age old feline ancestry –
They know how fleeting life is.
But cannot know the agony of loss,
Console, console, life's ending is but a beginning –
Time will heal, but some small part of me has also died,
Looking at his vacant chair.

Death of Bill
November 18th 1994

THE ULTIMATE DREAM

There's the road, stretching endlessly
Upwards, onwards towards infinity.
The human race walks on this way,
All men and women, some limping, some running;
Some smiling, some crying, some singing,
Some with solemnity, some with joy.
Little paths lead off and onto the major way,
For many will divert and join again,
And a few will wander off in pain,
Lost, bewildered, tired and worn,
Till Christ the Shepherd leads them to the dawn.
And some will cry 'there's no way out';
And some will sing and march and shout!
And others dance and sway and clap,
They've found the way and need no map,
While others walk with steadfast tread,
Their psalms and chanting fill the air,
For others will join in quietly with prayer,
It matters little to one who holds the key,
The celestial city is for all to see.
At the end of the road stands our Shepherd King –
With flowing robe and crown of thorns.
His hand will stretch out to greet them home,
Pilgrim welcome – journeys end.
He'll take no count of type of worship then.
Each one came along salvation's road,
Each one bore their different load,
For unity is now the ultimate goal realised,
A united sound will fill the skies,
At one with Christ, to sing in endless praise,
What sound will thrill, as anthems raise.

February 14th 1995

THEY SHALL NOT GROW OLD

I heard today of the death of an old man,
So what! He had already reached his allotted span,
I looked at the Queen bearing flowers for grief,
I could not weep, I cannot comprehend
The death of innocents; the empty void
Left by the empty bedroom of a child.
I have no grief in my ageing years
To match the sorrow left behind.
But I have prayed and seen Christ walk,
A King of Sorrows, with hands outstretched to bless,
And heal the bitterness and sudden loss.
The old man died – he's now at rest,
Life's span done – and heaven blest.
Then the image of the children came
So clearly – they were laughing and playing
In meadows awash with flowers –
The light was bright – the angels sang
Ring-a-roses; they pick daisies in heaven
And are happy; yes mourn and cry
But let Christ in – your children are safe,
Safe in the everlasting arms of God.

The Children of Dunblane
March 18th 1996

HOPE FOR THE NEW YEAR

Another new year, what will it bring?
Just look for the signs of approaching spring;
It's dull, it's dreary, the start of the year,
With wintry sunshine, darkening days.
Perhaps snow will gently mask the hills
And icicles slope and frost bite sills –
Soon our world will be enveloped in white,
Winter wonderland makes a magic sight –
Traffic noise is muted, and all seems still,
Motions slow; and coldness saps our very will –
For we are forced to slow life's hectic pace,
Which gives time to reflect on the human race.
So we have a landscape purified
In white, to start a brand new year,
And when melting snows disappear,
The first, tender shoots of spring appear,
For it's never too late to wipe the slate
And make a new beginning –
For as nature shows, under the snows,
The first snowdrop shows.

January 1997

SUMMER'S ANTICIPATION

Now summer sun on us descends –
And all bird song with nature blends –
Happiness! For wintry winds have long gone away,
We are alert and blessed for the first of May.
We dream on, our miseries depart,
Think of pleasures and take heart.
First go quietly to a secret place,
Where once quiescent bulbs did hide their face.
Now bluebells shimmer there beneath the trees.
For in drifts their colour catches the breeze.
Their swathes of blue have a mystic shine,
Their scent with magic fills the air like wine.
Soon Exbury will be ablaze with pinks and reds,
As rhododendrons raise their heads
In huge bushes bright with bloom,
Go in May, there's plenty of room.
Then take walks by the river's way,
Where gentle breezes and trout will play.
The swans will proudly parade as well,
And ducks and ducklings bob in water's swell.
Still in the New forest there is peace,
Away from crowds, and traffic still does cease
In the heart of the forest, under great trees,
Tread softly, for the deer with delicate tread
Drink by the dewpond, new foals lift their head,
With unsteady legs and bat-like ears,
And stand in the shade when high sun appears.
So on through the summer days,
Anticipation comes with the sun's rays.
Sit in the garden, swim in the sea,
Strawberries and cream, a sun-hat for me.
Enjoy the moments for memories are made
In summer days and do not fade
When winter comes.

April 8th 1997

DEATH OF A PRINCESS

Flowers strew her place,
Candles light her face,
Pictures show her grace,
What a tragic waste!

We watched her grow through 16 years,
And felt her happiness and tears.
She became part of our fears
For her innovative ways.

For first she became a fashion plate,
That men might love or women hate,
Or envy her beauty and her fate –
But another character emerged.

We saw her elegant and neat,
And then her smile as she would greet
And touch the ones with crippled feet,
And turn despair to hope.

For she became the spirit of our age,
Showing compassion, becoming sage
Beyond her years; for she would wage
A campaign for the underdog.

We watched her walking through a minefield,
For as she touched, so she healed,
But with her unconventional ways, her fate was sealed,
And so suddenly she died.

Sleep, the world discarded,
Sleep, unregarded,
Your deeds, rewarded,
The Prince of Peace will bless you.

R.I.P. Diana
September 6th 1997

THE SECRET GARDEN

Who walked in the dew dappled light alone,
Beyond the guardian gate?
The gate invites to look beyond
Into wonderland – a secret place.
So open quietly, and with awe,
Ignore the creak, as never before…
Not for years – break the spell –
Do not destroy what is there.
Tangled roses on a bower.
Honeysuckle scent on long grasses.
Quiet as the grave – peace intangible .
An old stone seat – where lovers sat?
Once a path led onwards
To the lake – now reed bound,
Old yellow irises surround.
Birds still there, calling from the trees,
That sigh and bend in summer breeze-
Their only sound to break the spell-
Walk softly – breathe slow –
If you turn your head, they're there.
The lovers sit still on the seat.
Her muslin dress flowing to the ground.
She listens as he bends his head –
To whisper soft as summer breeze –
'I love you, Beth – forever – ever'
The wind shakes the leaves – they're gone.
Quietly retrace your steps –
Take one deep breath of scents of old.
Open the gate, and go back to now.
Leave them to love, eternally young.

June 1999

NOVEMBER

Now November is here
It's dark, it's drear
The dregs of the year
Can I escape?

Trees are bare now
Their carpet is laid
Their leaves have made
A golden swirl.

Soon fireworks will light the sky
And chestnuts roast and bye and bye
The sun will glimmer with a sigh
And so shall I.

The hedgerows will sleep,
The sky will weep,
Frost's cold fingers creep.
A dismal time.

The holly will soon be clothed in red,
Its berries glow, all is not dead,
Hope rears its head
So do not cry.

Angels will tell of glad new birth,
Carols will be sung on earth,
And children will laugh with mirth;
And so shall I.

November 1999

THE BOOK OF THE WORLD

Let the bells ring out,
Let a million candles burn.
Millennium! Millennium!
What does it mean?
That 2000 years ago or thereabouts –
A babe was born –
The oxen sighed –
The shepherds knelt –
The wisemen came and angels sang.
One tiny babe – The Light of the World was born.

Throughout the years of sweat and toil,
Through pestilence and plague –
Through wars and threats of wars –
Through joy and tears of men,
Through our scientific, computer,
Internet and television age,
A single fact still remains,
Like candlelight flicker in a power-cut world –
That our saviour Christ was born in Bethlehem.

The pages of the book of the world will turn,
Another chapter done, and time moves on –
Our little minds cannot comprehend
The vastness of eternity and what will be,
In this bright new century –
The pages still have to be written,
And we who sent man to the moon,
Are powerless to tell of what will be,
But God surely knows and He will reveal,
Then the candlelight flicker will burn brighter
Than a thousand, thousand suns
When Christ returns again.

January 2000